I0532437

This book belongs to:_____

Date:_____

Mastering & Manifesting Your Promised Land Within!

Volume II

WORDOLOGY

Sticks & Stones Might Break My Bones But Words Will Definitely Harm Me!

PHYLLIS V. WHITLEY

COPYRIGHT

Printed in the United States of America.
Self Whisper, LLC PhyllisWhitley.com
WhisperVise Inc. WhisperVise.org
ISBN: 979-8-9879970-5-5

DEDICATION

This book is dedicated to all my clients and mentees who allowed me to revise their broken words (whispers) into voices of victory.

*In the beginning was the **Word**, and the Word was with God, and the Word was God. He was in the beginning with **God**. All things were made through Him, and without Him nothing was made that was **made**.*

John 1:1-3 (NKJV)

TABLE OF CONTENTS

PREFACE

The proverb "sticks and stones may break my bones" is said to have its initial traces in 1844, in Alexander William Kinglake's book, where it is used as "golden sticks and stones." Later, it was cited in The Christian Recorder of March, published in 1862, where it was stated; "sticks and stones may break my bones, but words will never break me."

It also appeared in 1872 in Mrs. George Cupples's piece, Tappy's Chicks: and Other Links Between Nature and Human Nature, where it is stated; "Sticks and stones may break my bones / But names will never harm me." (Sticks And Stones May Break My Bones-LiteraryDevices. https://literarydevices.net/sticks-and-stones-may-break-my-bones/).

Unlike the other proverbs mentioned, my sayings are that "sticks and stones might break my bones, but words will definitely harm me." For centuries, believers failed to notice that words can cause significant damage. Words are powerful, as they create your world. You will see, or experience, manifestations of what was once said by you or someone who spoke into your five senses that are still haunting you to this day. Those words continue to play over and over in your head (within your mind) every day.

Millions of dollars are spent annually on counseling sessions, depression medication, and divorce courts due to words that considerably harm people. Unfortunately, it can be as simple as damaged phrases or just one specific word that tears down a person from within, causing them to attract a world of chaos filled with empty words of "why" or "how" until death.

Yes, words are like seeds planted in the field, which is your mind, and they either grow into beautiful flowers or deadly weeds that can sting your life growth, cancel out your true destiny, and keep you from your true heart's desire called promised land.

CHAPTER 1

IF THIS WORLD WERE MINE

(Song Artist Luther Vandross & Cheryl Lynn)

Words Create Worlds:

You might ask how I can create my world. First, you must know that your words are seeds sown into your five senses daily and need to be **revised** and watched over daily. For example, what do you whisper to yourself every day?

Do you repeatedly hear the traumatic words someone spoke to you years ago? Notice the things I mentioned can't be seen with the naked eye unless you write on paper or type them out to become visible. Where are these things?

They exist in the invisible world and manifest into the visible world where your five senses can witness it. If your world is overloaded with crazy relationships, career, or financial drama, then take note of how much time you spend watching reality drama shows and late-night news. Maybe you are listening to your friends and family talk to you about all the wrongs in their relationships.

Stop the lack in your life by focusing on how you can improve yourself throughout your day instead of worrying about what is lacking in your life. Learn how to spend your time wisely on people, places, and things that elevate you and release what hurts you.

I am talking about protecting your spiritual world because everything is created first in this hidden, unseen **world**, and all the junk words you allow to be planted in your mind are like a seed planted in your garden's dirt.

Gospel Truth:

According to Genesis 1, God created the heavens and earth, in the beginning, from a formless and empty covering of darkness over the water through his words. As they **manifested** *(appeared), he named them.*

Next, God **created** *vegetation, day, night, and living & crawling creatures for the sky, sea, and land. Finally, God created man in His image, which is spirit, because God is spirit, and He blessed everything, and He rested on the Seventh day of His work of creation.*

Prophetic Secret:

When God was creating the world, He made every living creature seed-bearing, so it is no wonder he commanded it all to **multiply** because only a seed can reproduce according to its kind.

In short, if you don't like your world, try changing it from within. Seeds can be your thoughts, imagination, and words.

Remember that your word is a seed that multiplies into your world, whether good or bad, creating your future world. In the same manner, men were made from dirt, so what you plant in your soil will grow and is formed into your visible physical world each time. So, change your world by planting good **seeds**!

MEDITATION QUOTE

"Change your world by planting good seeds."

PHYLLIS Y. WHITLEY

SELF-REFLECTION NOTES

CHAPTER 2

YOU STUPID FOOL

(Song Artist Dee 1)

Words Create Ignorance:

During the **slavery era**, it was forbidden for slaves to read and write, leaving them at the mercy and total dependency of their masters, making it a crime for others to teach them.

Southern slave states enacted anti-literacy laws between 1740 and 1834 prohibiting enslaved and free people of color from reading, writing, or being taught. If any of them attempted to break this law, they were severely punished for literacy crimes with vicious beatings to the removal of limbs.

The slavery system of Anti-literacy gave slave masters, even the illiterate masters, complete control, and power. The **illusion** of white supremacy was on their side because they used these secrets to keep slaves and free people of color in ignorance by taking their rights to read or write.

Ignorance was a part of slaves' life as they suffered physical and mental punishment like a beast to reduce us to what they wanted us to be: stupid. A plan was created to keep slaves producing generational ignorance for centuries to come and a legacy that's consistently destroying black people to date.

The **anti-literacy** mission was accomplished. Slave masters increased in power and control, while black people increased in ignorance.

This is important today because your ancestors were forced into obliviousness. Many were killed trying to learn to read. What is your excuse?

Gospel Truth:

Why are we counted as beasts, and regarded as stupid in your sight? (Job 18:3).

The lips of the righteous nourish many, but fools die for lack of sense. (Proverbs 10:21).

Whoever loves instruction loves knowledge, But he who hates correction is stupid. Proverbs 12:1 (NKJV).

Prophetic Secret:

The lack of **words** creates **ignorance**. Do you get the picture yet? Slavery created the ignorant seeds that pass through each generation to keep people of color out of power and out of control in their life. Stop walking in the stigma of your ancestors who had no choice.

Reverence your freedom today and take your power back by feeding yourself with words through reading and writing the rest of your life.

Read to your unborn child during pregnancy, teach your children to read before they start school, incorporate reading and writing rewards in your home, learn to write your own books, build a library in your home office, and teach your children to write their own **books**. Don't allow your future generation to die from a lack of sense.

Every secret you need to know about is in words written in books you refuse to read. Words were taken away from your ancestors to keep them in **ignorance**. Not one person or system can stop you today because the last time I checked the library was free.

Whether you choose to go to a Library branch or online, you have access to free hidden treasure. Those treasures are the secrets to your family living in its promised land today and your guide to leaving a wise **legacy** for tomorrow.

MEDITATION QUOTE

"As long as the library is free; read enormously"

PHYLLIS Y. WHITLEY

SELF-REFLECTION NOTES

CHAPTER 3

BROKE

(Song Artist Lecrae)

Words Create Poverty:

Have you ever been in poverty or known people living beneath their means? If your answer is yes, I want you to look at their environment and speech. What do you see and hear? Lack!

For example, most people in poverty talk about bad drama, their scarcity, or excuses which are weapons for destroying their environment through crime, leaving education an unappealing or non-conversation piece.

According to PovertyUSA.org, Native Americans, blacks, and Hispanics are among the highest poverty level in the United States. There are many reasons these groups have a high poverty rate. For instance, black children lack parental support, attend overcrowded schools, and experience high levels of peer pressure.

Native Americans have impoverished economic reservations and Hispanics have language barriers. Yes, these might be statistical facts but let's look at the root cause of poverty: insufficient education. Your education or specialization increases the words that develop your mind and not decline it to the wrong address.

It's important to know that some of the wealthiest countries like Luxembourg, Norway, Germany, Singapore, Denmark, Switzerland, and Finland also have the most educated population. Note that there is a strong link between wealth and education.

You might argue the fact that wealth allowed them to afford education, but what if your education can bring your wealth? Would you value education more? Or suppose I told you that education can change your address, will you make it a priority for you and your kids?

Gospel Truth:

*The hypocrite with his mouth destroys his neighbor, but through **knowledge**, the righteous will be delivered.*
Proverbs 11:9

*The tongue of the wise use's **knowledge** rightly, But the mouth of fools pours forth foolishness.*
Proverbs 15:2

Prophetic View:

It starts with your **poverty consciousness** (mindset). When you feed your mind with good words, and good news, and understand the value of education for you and your family, you will eliminate excuses, receive knowledge, and close the door of foolishness.

For this same reason, so many cultures prioritize **education** because they know it's not only the secret to their family's success but the **secret** to breaking their poverty cycle.

In short, education uses knowledge to build words that create books, magazines, contracts, inventions, relationships, podcasts, and movies that will soon replace poverty with **prosperity** guaranteed to change your **address** from a ghetto lane to an extraordinary boulevard called your promised land.

MEDITATION QUOTE

"Education increases words that develop your mind."

PHYLLIS Y. WHITLEY

SELF-REFLECTION NOTES

CHAPTER 4

SOMEBODY LIED TO US

(Song Artist Sevin / Hog Mob
Ministries)

Words Create Gossip:

The wrong words can create **gossip** when you allow yourself to believe another person's lies, even if they are dead or still alive. The danger is when you feel these lies about others or yourself.

According to dictionary.com *Gossip* is **idle** talk or reports about other people, typically involving details that are not confirmed as being true. In other words, what report will you believe?

Have you ever had someone tell you something about someone else that you knew was false, but you still took their word for the truth? Maybe your loved one said something false about you to others or in your face? Whether it was a stranger, a loved one, or your so-called friend, your world turned into a gossip column you chose to believe.

People can say anything to you, but when you allow their words to sink into your **subconscious** mind like a seed growing in your garden or field, you will become a doubting Thomas listening to every word that passes you.

Gossip will keep you from your promised land and drive you into a gossip land that causes confusion and **manifests** a life of regret, revenge, and rivals, leaving you no choice but to settle on the wrong ground. For example:

- When you dream of a college degree, but settle for a high school diploma.
- You **settle** for a spouse who abuses you because someone told you this was real love.
- You settle for living in the hood or projects when you dreamed of buying a home.
- You agree to socialize with cool and the **gang** when you are an intelligent, cool nerd.
- You settle for a minimum wage job because someone laughs at your ideals of owning your own business.

Gospel Truth: (NKJV)

*According to Genesis 3, before Eve was **created** from Adam's ribs, God had already commanded Adam not to eat the tree of knowledge due to the results of death.*

*Although Adam conveyed this message to Eve, the valid message got twisted around when Eve listened and believed the **lies** the cunning serpent told her that were just **gossip**. Soon after, they both ate the fruit of that tree. Unfortunately, that lie causes them* *both to be kicked out of God's presence, their promised land, to live as **limited** mortals on this finite earth leaving the next generations to come searching for their promised land all over again.*

Prophetic View:

After eating the fruit from the tree of knowledge against God's command, Adam and Eve's eyes were opened, and they knew they were naked. Genesis 3:7. (NKJV).

Could it be that the tree of **knowledge** of good & evil enabled them to see corruption, or should I say lack? Yes, neither one noticed they lacked something until they ate the **fruit**.

In short, the serpent is any person, place, or thing that brings gossip and lies to you to keep you out of your promised land, so believe what God says about you, learn from Mother Eve, and **beware** of the **gossip**.

MEDITATION QUOTE

*"Gossip will keep you from your promised land
and drive you into gossip land."*

PHYLLIS Y. WHITLEY

SELF-REFLECTION NOTES

CHAPTER 5

I GOT THAT

(Song Artist Anthony Brown)

Words Create Fear:

Because **fear** is a distressing emotion aroused by impending danger, evil, pain, etc., whether the threat is real or imagined, it has stopped many people from pursuing their lifetime dream (dictionary.com).

As an adult, did you ever stop and think about the real reason why you are stuck in life and why you never pursued your childhood **dreams**?

Let's go back in memory lane. Please sit down, take a deep breath, and slowly remember when your mother caught your father cheating, when your teachers labeled you dumb, when your neighbor laughed at your dreams of moving out of the ghetto, your friends called you fat, your siblings called you ugly, and your boss laughed at your dreams of owning your own business.

Now, how did it feel to take a trip in the past? If all you remember are the hurtful **words** someone once said to you, you might still be feeling angry, regretful, and frustrated.

You might even say, "the past is the past." If that is true, then why are you living a life of excuses and walking in fear today from a past **threat** or an imagined pain:

- You avoid commitment because your father cheated on your mother.
- You wear baggy clothes to hide your figure because you believe you are shapeless.
- You are comfortable working for someone else, so you avoid starting your own business.
- You went on every diet there is even though you are not fat.
- You are needy in all your relationships because of your insecurities.
- You are fearful of buying a home, so instead, you settle for an apartment in the same ghetto your parents lived in.

Yes, you allow other people to crush your dreams because you believed their **report** about yourself as a child, which is dictating your adult life and paralyzing your dreams. Start dreaming again by flipping your world of fear into a world of faith.

Gospel Truth: (NKJV)

For the thing I greatly feared has come upon me, And what I dreaded has happened to me. Job 3:25

*For God has **not** given us a spirit of **fear**, but of power and of love and of a sound mind. 2 Timothy 1:7*

Prophetic View:

Walking in a spirit of Fear will **manifest** all the horrible things you fear as it did for Job 3:25. Therefore the masses of people are walking in weakness, hate, and a confused mind that strays them from their life dreams.

In short, Fear attracts weakness, hate, and a confused mind, while fearlessness **attracts power**, love, and a stable spirit so you can enjoy making your dreams come to **fruition**.

MEDITATION QUOTE

"Fearlessness attracts power, love, and a stable spirit to manifest your dreams."

PHYLLIS Y. WHITLEY

SELF-REFLECTION NOTES

CHAPTER 6

THIS IS WAR

(Song Artist Hi-Rez & Jimmy Levy)

Words Create Wars:

There are many types of wars, both small and large, some with intense **armed conflict** characterized by extreme violence, destruction, and mortality to a state or country using military forces (https://en.wikipedia.org/wiki/War). Other wars will bring destruction on the street using gang violence and domestic war in the home using verbal or physical abuse.

All wars start from within and are usually a manifesting of years of a silent killer that is often a valuable point but overlooked because it's the major unseen root cause for any type of war called "**Words**."

A war between a state or government is words of disagreement & power, the war in the neighborhood streets is an exchange of fighting words & control, and wars at the Homefront are words of slander & narcissism. Unseen words will always embody themselves into physical reality called war from speeches, contracts, texting, gossip, thoughts, letters, documents, messages, tweets, or phone calls.

Gospel Truth: *(NKJV)*

My tongue is the pen of a ready writer. (Psalms 45:1)

Who plan evil things in their hearts; They continually gather for war (Psalm 140:2).

Death and life are in the power of the tongue, and those who love it will eat its fruit. Proverbs 18:21

Prophetic View:

What can you **undo** when the tools you used yesterday expressed your words and left a permanent mark that can't be erased? **Revising** your broken words expressed from your tongue today through **visualization**, meditation, and affirmation will start a chain of good effects that will begin manifesting peace & **repair** in your world tomorrow.

MEDITATION QUOTE

"Use the power of your tongue to write your promised land."

PHYLLIS Y. WHITLEY

SELF-REFLECTION NOTES

CHAPTER 7

NOT FOR SALE

(Song Artist Bizzle w/Lauryn Hill)

Words Create Abuses:

Verbal abuse, also known as emotional abuse, is the manifestation of consistent harmful words that are expressed in a tragic or harmful way. And by now, if you are not convinced that words can harm, then it may shock or surprise you to hear that emotional abuse may include, but are not limited to, **hostile** remarks, verbal attacks, threats, taunts, intimidation, and being unsupportive. (American Nurses Association, 2015).

Emotional abuse could cause long-term damage if the harsh words were from loved ones or important people in your life, such as your parents, teacher, boss, or spiritual leader.

Their words can also cause you to second guess your ability to move forward and become successful in life because your scars will become a rerun show playing in your mind throughout your life.

Unfortunately, hurtful words could become contagious, especially if the painful word started in childhood at the **bullying** playground, where if not resolved as a child might become a lifetime therapy session as an adult.

Understanding how multiple harmful words can produce major havoc in one's life will begin the process to prevent tragic outcomes that will manifest into verbal abuse, if not, become revised by wise counsel.

Gospel Truth: (NKJV)

Teach me, and I will hold my tongue; Cause me to understand wherein I have erred. Job 6:24
A wholesome tongue is a tree of life, but perverseness in it breaks the spirit. Proverbs 15:4
The words of a man's mouth are deep waters; The wellspring of wisdom is a flowing brook. Proverbs 18:4

Prophetic View:

A tongue of **wisdom** should be taught in the home first with the understanding that your tongue must be tamed to have a happy **spirit** and a successful life. Learning the power of your words and how they can change someone's life to a brook of overflowing wisdom or words that will keep a person at the bottom of the well of failure.

In short, the best **gift** you can give anyone is a word of wisdom that will automatically feed their spirit life & truth!

MEDITATION QUOTE

"If not revised by wise counsel, multiple hurtful words will manifest into verbal abuse."

PHYLLIS Y. WHITLEY

SELF-REFLECTION NOTES

CHAPTER 8

DIVINE INTERVENTION

(Song Artist Lecrae)

Words Create Sickness:

In Humans, the disease is often used more broadly to refer to any condition that causes **pain** or death, (https://www.publichealth.com.ng/types-of-diseases/). Inappropriately, the medical communities usually prescribe **medicine** that temporarily suppresses the pain with terrible side effects, long-term drug dependency, and unanswered death. All due to the wrong healing focus and a quick fix that continues to put millions in the pharmaceutical marketplace.

On the other hand, the **holistic** approach is described as treating the whole person, considering mental and social factors rather than just sickness **symptoms**. This approach will visit the root cause of the dis-easement of a person's mental and social aspects.

Which can reveal unforgiveness, regrets, hatred, and low self-esteem that need repairing before it manifests in pain and **dis-easement** become detrimental to a person's health if overlooked.

Above all, since most of these factors are invisible with no claims of curing any disease but a possible cause for sickness; let's look at the spiritual seeds of broken words that will create a chain of effects if not **pruned** during a person's lifetime. Yes, words can play a significant role in a person's life, especially if they were broken words traveling through your spiritual expression as pain or, should I say, dis-easement.

Gospel Truth: (NKJV)

*The spirit of a man will sustain him in **sickness**, but who can bear a broken spirit? Proverbs 18:14*

*So that even handkerchiefs or aprons were brought from his body to the sick, and the **diseases** left them, and the evil spirits went out of them. Acts 19:12*

Prophetic View:

If a man's spirit is sick, it's broken words that invaded his or her body throughout their five senses.

Evil means wrong, immoral, harmful, and detrimental, according to dictionary.com. Therefore, in Acts 19:12, evil spirits (broken words) went out of them, and their diseases left them. Diseases or sickness cannot stay in a body when that spirit is released from broken words.

In short, diseases or sicknesses cannot stay in a body when that spirit is released from evil or should I say, "broken words".

MEDITATION QUOTE

""Heal your broken spirit and watch sicknesses abandon your body.".

PHYLLIS Y. WHITLEY

SELF-REFLECTION NOTES

CHAPTER 9

DON'T WASTE YOUR LIFE

(Song Artist Lecrae)

Words Create Laziness:

Words of discouragement and labels from parents, friends, teachers, and bullies put into a child's mind are among the many factors that create a **slothful** spirit. Laziness might be one of the biggest surprises whispered, causing many to ask, how can words cause someone to become lazy in the world?

Although in some instances, "**lazy**" might be considered inactive physically when it comes down to the spiritual side of man, it can be an idle mind that will manifest into a slack or stagnant life production.

Sadly, the rotten **seed** of negligent words starts in childhood when a parent is too soft on their sons and daughters by not giving them the responsibility that will challenge their minds along with physical activity, chores, or hobbies that will keep their body conditioned.

Too often, parents leave all the work to their child's teacher, but it all starts in the womb to childhood with "**words**" in songs, pictures, sounds, and talk. In other words, **create** a Godly, motivational, and positive talk environment around your home for your children's minds to avoid an adult life full of indolent excuses; someone who is lazy, not wanting to work or making any effort to do anything.

Gospel Truth: (NKJV)

*The soul of a lazy man **desires** and has nothing, But the soul of the diligent shall be made rich. Proverbs 13:4*

*He who is **slothful** in his work Is a brother to him who is a great destroyer. Proverbs 18:9*

*Train up a **child** in the way he should go, And when he is old he will not depart from it. Proverbs 22:6*

Prophetic View:

When the bible refers to a **diligent** soul, it's the same as an active spirit that attracts wealth choices. Teaching your children the correct spiritual protocol of excellent words will prevent the enemy of laziness from manifesting their minds into **idleness**, an adult destroyer that wants to keep your whole generation out of their promised land.

In short, a busy mind will keep your butt out of the poverty line.

MEDITATION QUOTE

"A busy mind will keep you out off the poverty line."

PHYLLIS Y. WHITLEY

SELF-REFLECTION NOTES

CHAPTER 10

SEASONS

(Song Artist Hillsong Worship)

Words Create Seeds:

God created the world with his words, and since we are made in the image of Him, we must create our world through what God said about us. What happens to all the other **traumatizing** words that are implanted into us through our five senses from other people? These broken words turn into seeds like farmers planting them in their fields, but in our case, the fields are our minds.

It's safe to say that not all words turn into a seed that grows, so what about the ones that grow? It will manifest in our world. Words that ripen determine our fruit, whether good or **rotten**, so we must recognize and prune those awful words daily, or they will sting and paralyze our growth to be the version of ourselves if we don't learn the truth that will set us free.

Gospel Truth: (NKJV)

*"A sower went out to sow his seed. And as he sowed, some fell by the **wayside**; and it was trampled down, and the birds of the air devoured it. Some fell on **rock**; and as soon as it sprang up, it withered away because it lacked moisture.*

*And some fell among thorns, and the thorns sprang up with it and choked it. But others fell on good **ground**, sprang up, and yielded [a]a crop a hundredfold." When He had said these things He cried, "He who has ears to **hear,** let him hear! Then His disciples asked Him, saying, "What does this parable mean? And He said, "To you it has been given to know the [b]mysteries of the kingdom of God, but to the rest it is given in parables, that 'Seeing they may not see, And hearing they may not understand." Luke 8:5-10.*

Prophetic View:

Every word that comes into our life is either God's words (**God-spell**) or everybody else's bad words (bad spells, curses, seeds). The devil (doubt) is any person outside of us who dropped a word that opposed God's word about your true **self**.

In short, cultivating the seeds sown in your mind, body, and spirit will **manifest** your harvest season.

MEDITATION QUOTE

"Choose the seeds that try to fertilize your spiritual ground."

PHYLLIS Y. WHITLEY

SELF-REFLECTION NOTES

CONCLUSION

*For the word of God is living and **powerful**, and **sharper** than any **two-edged sword**, **piercing** even to the division of soul and spirit, and of joints and marrow, and is a **discerner** of the **thoughts** and intents of the **heart**.*

Hebrews 4:12 (NKJV)

THE WORD

*Come hear me **roar** and keep me in your heart*

Until death do us part,

I will feed and nurture you for this reason

With patience, my fruits shall yield in due season,

*When you finally **express** yourself outside of me*

My secret will be manifested for all to see,

The devil doesn't care if you can hear or see

*He just doesn't want you to grow **within** me,*

Because he knows he lost the war at Cavalry

Oh, yes, I am your word you need to cultivate and

continue to believe,

*They call me "**SEED**"*

AFFIMATION THERAPY

*At this moment, I **release** all the words of lack &*

ignorance implanted in my subconscious mind. I

now receive my sacred place, divine connection,

and divine protection that brings me divine Glory

of abundance in my blessed rightful time.

*Unexpected and delayed blessings are **pouring** on*

my household, career, mind, health, self-image,

and ideas powerfully.

*Fearlessness **awakens** my spiritual discernment*

in all my daily transactions and activities,

knowing that my gift makes room for me.

I shall not want because my divine Father

*promised me a land filled with **milk and honey**.*

I am a tree of life creating my own life play within,

so I choose whom to fire or hire at my Father's

commands.

*II cut out weeds of debt, doubt, or division sown in my field of consciousness daily and prune all the **illusions** of destruction planted in my inner soul.*

__Meditation__ is my claim to step over all my hindrances, obstacles, lies, and lacks. I use them as my anchor to motivate me to see my miracles and my accurate facts.

*I no longer waste my God-given talents as I now feel, walk and talk until I witness a reflection that **manifests** my excellency.*

I soak in laughter, humbleness, and wisdom as I yield good fruits.

*At last, I see myself as divine Glory sees me (a person who can). Now I must get busy as I teach and help others reach thei unique mountain top called **promised** land.*

Thank you, Supreme Glory, Within!

SELF-WHISPER EXERCISE

1. Looking back on when you were a child, what did you want to be when you grew up?

2. Name up to ten reality dreams you had growing up (career, real estate, business, relationship, finance, family?

3. What lies & incorrect beliefs were installed in you as a child?

4. How many dreams did you stop believing in?

5. How many dreams did you accomplish and change to date?

6. What person, place, or thing were your dream killers?

7. What are your new/revised dreams after reading this book?

SELF-WHISPER EXERCISE

8. After reading this book, list your dream goals and the timeframe to achieve them.

9. What character in the bible best describes the old you?

10. What prophet or book in the bible best describes the new you?

11. What does your promised land look like now?

12. Write your own poem about new life (consciousness).

Prayer

Thank you, Father. I now know who you are and who I am in you. I am free of bondage because of your son, Lord Jesus, who set an example for my family and me.

Therefore, I release and let go of those who trespassed against me and those whom I trespassed against. I now know that my power is within me; therefore, I no longer fear those things outside myself because you walk with me and talk to me daily.

Father, I promise to use my knowledge, talent, and gifts to please you always and forever with order and a respectful protocol to all those spiritual leaders called by You for your purpose.

I shall not want any good thing because my family and I cup are running over with prosperity for all the days of our lives and unto the next generations that will be called blessed.

Verily, verily, I say unto you, He that believeth on me, the works that I do shall he do also; and greater works than these shall he do.
John 14:12 (KJV).

⚜ABOUT THE AUTHOR⚜

Phyllis Y. Whitley was born and raised in the Bronx, NY. She is the CEO and founder of SelfWhisper, LLC, and the nonprofit organization WhisperVise, Inc. Phyllis graduated as a Certified Holistic Health Coach from the Institute for Integrative Nutrition. In addition, she has a Bachelor of Science in Psychology and Religion Studies and a Master of Arts in Human Service/Wellness from Liberty University.

The go-to relationship guru since the days of her teens, Phyllis discovered her passion for helping women overcome relationship drama. Then, at age 26, she gave her life to Christ and began a personal discovery of another type of pain called Church Hurt from shepherd slaughtering.

Through her journey, Phyllis quickly learned that God desires to bless us holistically (mind, body, and soul) so we can do His work in the marketplace while living in our promised land.

A conqueror of cancer, Phyllis overcame many years of religious bondage and lack and uses her experience from those past pains to help guide others into a voice of victory. An Ordained Minister and a Prophetess, she prefers to walk by God's truth and not her titles, as she uses her education, skills, and experiences to empower and deliver people from religious bondage, relationship abuse, and the lies that come with it.

Phyllis represents herself using a sweet-smelling rose born out of her broken whispers, a meaningful symbol throughout her brands.

Phyllis is a sought-after holistic relationship consultant, prophetic teacher, visionary writer, mystic podcaster, and motivational speaker. She keeps it real and raw for her clients as she helps revise their broken, victimized whispers of yesterday so they can live in their promised land today.

She gifts her time teaching and building prophetic prayer warriors and Christ-conscious leaders by her example. Phyllis now resides in the sunshine state of Florida with her only daughter Priscilla.

"Beloved, I pray that you may prosper in all things and be in health, just as your soul prospers." (3 John 1:2)

Books By Phyllis V. Whitley

Ask Jalen!
Whisper-Me Wisdom Journal
Whisper Me God's Colors
Whisper Me God's Colors II
Whisper-Me Journal for Podcaster
Self-Whisper Meditation Therapy & Devotional Poetry
Whisper-Me Journal for Women
Prophetic Whisper Boot Camp (PWBC)
Spiritology

Order Volume 1 now on Amazon!

Audiobook also available on Amazon Audible.